KU-113-312

ELGIN INTERNATIONAL

ELGIN INTERNATIONAL

Compiled By
MORAG PIRIE

ABERDEEN UNIVERSITY PRESS

First published 1985
Aberdeen University Press
A member of the Pergamon Group

© Morag Pirie 1985

British Library Cataloguing in Publication Data

Elgin International
  1. Elgin (Name)
  I. Pirie, Morag
  910   G105

  ISBN 0-08-032459-2
  ISBN 0-08-032452-5 (Pbk)

Printed in Great Britain
The University Press
Aberdeen

This book is dedicated to all the people world-wide, too numerous to mention individually, who helped make possible the publication of this book.

Special thanks to Moray District Council, Elgin, Scotland, for sponsoring printing costs.

This project was conceived with the objective of raising funds for the Elgin, Scotland, branch of UNICEF, who will receive all profits from the sale of Elgin International.

CONTENTS

Flexi Cover by Donald Rattray, Head of Art Department, Elgin Academy

Andrew Douglas Alexander Thomas Bruce, K.T., C.D., LL.D., D.Litt., D.L., J.P. 11th Earl of Elgin and 15th Earl of Kincardine

FOREWORD

How has it come about that I, the present Chief of the Name of Bruce, should write a foreword to a book of the importance of Elgin? Well, it is simple enough; for my predecessor, Edward Bruce, who was born in 1548, was, in the year 1583, granted the temporalities of the dissolved Monastery of Kinloss. This was, subsequently, five times confirmed and, in addition to the land so acquired, Edward Bruce had a seat in Parliament. In 1598 he went, with the Earl of Mar, as Ambassador to England on two occasions, and it was as a result of his careful preparations that the accession of King James VI to the English Throne was so quickly accomplished. Edward Bruce and his son, Thomas, were closely connected in England with both King James and his son King Charles. When, in 1633, King Charles came North for his Coronation in Scotland, he created his friend, Thomas Bruce (3rd Lord Bruce of Kinloss) an Earl, on 21 June 1633, at Holyrood House. Thomas chose the City of Elgin from which to take his title, as it was situated so close to his lands of Kinloss. Although these lands were soon to be sold, and the territorial link thus broken, subsequent Earls have maintained a warm relationship with the Lantern of the North.

This series of articles equally conspires to maintain just as warm and curious relationships. Several of the Elgins and Port Elgins mentioned in the text have become known to me after a visit in the last thirty years. Size does not always make for the ultimate, but quality does abound in all the places of the name of Elgin. I feel sure I speak for all who live in an Elgin, that we are proud and happy to have been so pleasurably brought together by Mrs. Pirie's noble persistence.

INTRODUCTION

Curiosity can be a very strong feeling, which if followed can lead you up many strange paths. My curiosity was aroused in 1978 after reading an article in the Northern Scot, written by a local man who wrote under the pseudonym 'Crimond'. Only one sentence of the article stuck in my mind — 'there are 35 Elgins in the world'. Over the weekend the thought kept returning, why should there be so many Elgins. Had some emigrants travelled to pastures new and named that place after their birthplace? By the end of the weekend I had to know and to this end I wrote to the Postmaster who supplied me with twenty one addresses — I wrote to them all. Perhaps if I had received replies to all my letters my curiosity would have been satisfied, but human nature being what it is, I received replies to only half. The Elgin Library was my next stop and after searching through all the atlases available, I discovered not 35 but 47 Elgins. Over the years I have corresponded and become friends with people from the five continents. The replies to my questions were not always the ones I expected and there are still some answers to be found. This book holds the answers to some of my questions and answers some of the many questions put to me.

Elgin	Victoria	Australia
Elgin Downs	Queensland	Australia
Elgin	Western Australia	Australia
Elgin Mountain	Western Australia	Australia
Elgin	Manitoba	Canada
Elgin	New Brunswick	Canada
Elgin	Nova Scotia	Canada
Elgin	Ontario	Canada
Elgin	Quebec	Canada
Port Elgin	Ontario	Canada
Elgin Mills	Ontario	Canada
Port Elgin	New Brunswick	Canada
Elgin County	Ontario	Canada
Elgin	Clarendon	Jamaica
Elgin Town	St. Anne	Jamaica
Elgin	Ashburton	New Zealand
Elgin	Gisborne	New Zealand
Elgin	Nuwara Eliya	Sri Lanka
Elgin Falls	Nuwara Eliya	Sri Lanka
Elgin Dagi Mountain		Turkey
Elgin	Alabama	U.S.A.
Elgin	Antrim County, Michigan	U.S.A.
Elgin	Arkansas	U.S.A.
Elgin	Arizona	U.S.A.
Elgin	Genesee County, Michigan	U.S.A.
Elgin	Illinois	U.S.A.
Elgin	Iowa	U.S.A.
Elgin	Kansas	U.S.A.
Elgin	Kershaw County, S. Carolina	U.S.A.
Elgin	Lancaster County, S. Carolina	U.S.A.
Elgin	Minnesota	U.S.A.
Elgin	Missouri	U.S.A.
Elgin	Montana	U.S.A.
Elgin	Nebraska	U.S.A.
Elgin	Nevada	U.S.A.
Elgin	New York	U.S.A.
Elgin	North Dakota	U.S.A.
Elgin	Ohio	U.S.A.
Elgin	Oregon	U.S.A.
Elgin	Ottowa County, Michigan	U.S.A.
Elgin	Pennsylvania	U.S.A.
Elgin	Talmage County, Michigan	U.S.A.
Elgin	Tennessee	U.S.A.
Elgin	Texas	U.S.A.
Elgin	Utah	U.S.A.
Elgin	Virginia	U.S.A.
Elgin	Washington	U.S.A.

Many of the Elgins in the U.S.A. are only POSTAL AGENCIES.

ELGIN, SCOTLAND

The city and Royal Burgh of Elgin is a picturesque town, which is situated in the fertile Laich of Moray, in the north east of Scotland.

There seem to be two schools of thought as to how the name Elgin was conceived. Prior to 1226 the town was named in the Chartulory of Moray as Helgyn. It is believed by some that the town was named after a Norwegian chief named Helgy, who served in the army of Sigurd, Earl of Orkney. However, although the Norsemen fought along the seaboard of north east Scotland, there is no proof that they settled this far inland. The second and most probable answer lies with the ancient Scots. The Scots came from Ireland and with them they brought their culture and language — Gaelic. To the ancient Scots, Ireland was thought of as a goddess called *Elg*, *Banb*, or *Erin*. *Elg* (nowadays *Eilg*) is the poetic name for Ireland, *in* means little and *Eilginn* may mean Little Ireland. In the past Elgin was known to Gaelic speakers as *Eilginn Mhoireibh* to distinguish it from Glenelg near Skye.

There may be some doubt as to why the town received its name but there is no doubt the town owed its early growth in beauty, learning and wealth to the Church.

During the reign of Alexander I, the Bishopric of Moray was founded, and from then until the reformation many fine ecclesiastical houses were built: the hospice of Maison Dieu; the churches of the Greyfriars and the Blackfriars; the House of the Brothers of St. Lazarus; the Leper House; the Chanonry; the houses of the clergy and the jewel of the Bishopric — the magnificent Cathedral. Following the consecration of the Cathedral in 1224, Bishop Andrew de Moray set into motion his plans for the great building. Architects and highly skilled tradesmen were employed to work with talented ecclesiasts and together they built the highly adorned cathedral that was the pride of Moray. Twice serious fires of unknown origin were to damage the building but it was a fire of known origin that was to break the heart of Bishop Alexander Bur in June, 1390. The Wolf of Badenoch — Alexander Stewart, Earl of Buchan and son of Robert II — raided Elgin with his followers and burned many church buildings, including the cathedral which they nearly destroyed. Over the next century the cathedral was restored to its former glory but in 1507 the central tower collapsed, seemingly due to poor workmanship. Rebuilding work on the new tower, which measured 198 feet in height, was finished by 1538 and the cathedral was thought to be the finest in Scotland.

Elgin Cathedral in 1538 from a print by John Grant *Courtesy: Elgin Library*

Sadly today only a beautiful ruin remains. With the coming of the reformation in 1560 the cathedral was abandoned and in 1567 the lead was stripped from the roof by order of the Privy Council. The lead was loaded

2

onto a ship bound for Holland, where it was to be sold, but it never reached its destination as the ship sank in the North Sea. Wind and rain played havoc with the fabric of the building over the years and religious fanatics helped with the destruction, until finally on Easter Sunday 1711, what remained of the tower fell down. For nearly one hundred years after this date the stones from the ruin were used by the people of the town to build houses etc. At the beginning of the 19th century the townspeople decided to preserve what was left of the great building. A stone wall was built around the ruin and a keeper was appointed, John Shanks, and it is thanks to him that many of the carved stones are preserved. He took to himself the task of clearing the cathedral of the rubbish of a century, and when he died he was buried in the cathedral grounds. A fitting epitaph was written by Lord Cockburn, "Who so reverences the Cathedral will respect the memory of this man".

Today the cathedral is looked after by the Scottish Department of Ancient Monuments; it is a peaceful place, which is visited by thousands of tourists each year, from home and abroad. Apart from the restored church of the Greyfriars, which is now occupied by the gentle Sisters of Mercy, very little is left of the former church buildings.

Pans Port and Cathedral — 1985 *Courtesy: The Northern Scot, Elgin*

3

In the years before the new housing estates were built in Bishopmill, Kings-mills, New Elgin, Pansport and South Lesmurdie, many families lived in the old houses, down the closes (lanes) off the High Street, Elgin's main thorough-fare.

There was a great sense of community in the old closes. They were referred to more by name than by number, Craigellachie, Ladyhill and the Red Lion, to name but a few. The closes came in various shapes, some long and narrow, others narrow at the entrance but opening up into a wide courtyard, with the entry to some being through arcaded buildings for which Elgin is noted. Due to a new road being built to by-pass the High Street, many of the old closes were demolished; a few however have been saved and after careful renovation now provide very attractive housing for senior citizens. The closes at the bottom of Ladyhill were among the first to be demolished but today new houses have been built there with other housing schemes planned nearby, to encourage people to return to the city centre.

From early days people have always lived at the bottom of Ladyhill. During the 11th century there was a fort on the hill which was later replaced by a royal castle, the ruins of which can still be seen. When King Duncan of Scotland was injured by MacBeth Mormaer of Moravia, in 1040, it is thought that he was brought to the fort on Ladyhill, where he died of his wounds. In 1135 during the reign of King Duncan's grandson, David I, a royal castle was built on the hill and many royal kings were to occupy it on hunting visits to Moray. As castles go, though, this one had a short life. The last king to visit the castle was probably the English King Edward I, 'Hammer of the Scots'. For three days in July 1296 the English flag was flown over Elgin. Edward had with him an army of several thousand warriors and knights. Local Barons and Chieftains paid homage to the English king but a year later, at the onset of the War of Independence, some of these same men joined the supporters of Sir William Wallace and destroyed the castle, so that when Edward returned in 1303 he had to live in the manse of one of the canons. Though the castle was destroyed, the chapel dedicated to 'Our Lady' was left intact and for hundreds of years was used by the townspeople. The hill takes its name from this chapel although, alas, nothing remains of the chapel today.

Down through the ages Elgin has had many Royal visitors, who in the early days after the destruction of the castle, lived in the King's House in the centre of town. The King's House was later named Thunderton House by the Dunbars of Thunderton. During the Rebellion of 1745, Bonnie Prince Charlie rested at Thunderton House before going on to the Battle of Culloden. The lady of the house, Mrs. Arradule, an ardent Jacobite, kept the sheets he slept on and left instructions with her servants that upon her death she was to be wrapped in the Prince's sheets. Her wishes were duly carried out.

The Prince of Wales and his brothers, Prince Andrew and Prince Edward were educated at Gordonstoun School, which is situated a few miles out of

4

town and the Queen and the Royal Family have been frequent visitors to Elgin. During these visits, however, the Queen did not reside in the town but with friends in the country. Her Majesty has attended morning service in St. Giles on occasion.

St Giles Church and War Memorial *Courtesy: Chris Ashe*

St. Giles, or the Muckle Kirk as it is commonly known, stands in the centre of town. The present church was built on the site of the old St. Giles in 1827–28, in the style of a Greek Doric temple and belongs to the Church of Scotland. Before the Reformation, the church would have belonged to the Roman Catholic Church but unlike the Cathedral which was not used for public worship, St. Giles was kept in use but under new management. St. Giles has a sister church, St. Columba's, which is situated at the south side of town. There are many beautiful Christian churches of all denominations in town and recently the Chinese built a new church in Bishopmill, to serve the needs of the Chinese Christian community.

Located at the west end of town, is the largest of Elgin's four hospitals, Dr. Gray's. The hospital was built in 1816-19, paid for by the generosity of a former son of Elgin who made a fortune in India. Dr. Alexander Gray left £20,000 to build the hospital "for the sick of the town and county of Elgin". The hospital is built in the classical style as is the old Academy, which now houses the Moray College of Education.

Education in Elgin today is provided by eight primary schools, two secondary schools and a community college. There is also specialist education for the mentally handicapped children and play groups for the under fives. The children commence school at age five and must remain in school until they reach sixteen, which is usually in the fourth year of secondary school. They may, however, remain at school until they complete their sixth year. On leaving school the young people have the choice of further education at college or university. Some leave the town to find work whilst the remainder look for employment in Elgin.

As far back as the 14th century Elgin has sought trade with the rest of the world. The Earl of Moray exported woollen cloth to the continent in 1393, and after the Reformation, when the merchants and trades had to look to sources other than the church for custom, a successful export trade with Holland and the continent was started. The Magistrates were granted the right to raise taxes on ale to build the town's own harbour at Elginhead (now Lossiemouth). Today Elgin is the business centre of the whisky industry, there being forty-nine stills in Moray district alone. The industrial estate at the east end of town houses many small service industries, supplying the whisky, farming and fishing industries, and in recent years the North Sea Oil Industry. A growing tourist industry is also well catered for; visitors can enjoy the best of Scottish cuisine and hospitality and visit many places of historic and scenic interest. The town has always been known for the quality of its merchandise and a few years ago the woollen mill received the Queens award for industry because of its excellent export trade in quality tweed and cashmere.

Elgin 1985 is a growing, bustling little city with a population of 19,500. The local industries still look to the international markets for their trade and like their ancestors before them find it in the Common Market and the world at large.

The children too are encouraged to be international in their outlook. They realise that there are other children in the world who need their help and are always happy to give it. The future of Elgin is safe with these caring young people who will carry on the international traditions of their antecedents.

A group of youngsters from the St Giles' Youth Fellowship, Elgin, Scotland, who took part in a sponsored 24 hours fast in the Church Hall to raise money for Christian Aid. Rev. Andrew Wilson (back right) organised the event. *Courtesy: Northern Scot, Elgin*

Greetings sent from Elgin, Scotland to Elgin Illinois, U.S.A. 1935

It is a matter of great interest to the Town Council and Community of the City and Royal Burgh of Elgin, Scotland, that one of our namesakes—Elgin, Illinois, U.S.A.—is this year celebrating its centenary as a city.

We are one of the five Cities of Scotland and this proud title is not due to our size or importance as a business community. Over 700 years ago, our Cathedral, now a stately ruin, was an established seat of light and learning amongst a rude and semi-barbarous people. The Lantern of the North is today an attraction to visitors from all over the world, even as a ruin.

Elgin, Scotland, is justly proud of her ancient and historic background and from our small city of 9,000 inhabitants, situated in a pleasant and salubrious part of the north east of Scotland, with centuries of tradition and example behind us, we congratulate our buxom daughter of Elgin, Illinois on having cut her first centennial tooth. May you flourish and prosper and ever keep your communal name fair and unsullied.

R.C. Hamilton
Lord Provost,
Elgin, Scotland.

Answer to Lord Provost's Message from Mayor Myron M. Lehman:

The Mayor and City Council of Elgin Illinois, wish to express its sincere appreciation for the splendid felicitations and message of goodwill brought to it by our friendly city in Bonnie Scotland. A happy concord between American and Scot still persists not only in solemn covenants but in indissoluble ties of friendship and mutual esteem.

ELGIN, ILLINOIS, U.S.A.

The founder of Elgin, Illinois, James Talcott Gifford, was born on the first day of the 19th century, in Herkimer, New York. His ancestors were English immigrants who settled in Massachusetts in the 17th century. When James was eleven years old his family moved to Sherburne, New York, where he received a good education and became a surveyor. As a surveyor he visited many southern states and his liking for southern architecture came to the fore when he later built his own beautiful house in Elgin. In 1834 James' brother, Hezekiah Gifford returned from the west where he had been looking for good land to farm. He persuaded James to sell the family farm and go back west with him. To this end, in February 1835, the brothers set out for Chicago, arriving there in early March and setting out on horseback the same day to find their promised land. On reaching the Fox River, they were ferried across by two Pottawatomie Indians, in canoes. In later years James took great pleasure in telling the story of how the Indians refused payment of one shilling by shaking their heads and saying 'Somma, Somma'. The brothers offered them more money but the Indians still declined the offer, and it was only after one of the Indians took a pipe out of his hair and again repeated 'Somma, Somma' that the brothers realised they wanted tobacco, which cost much less than the three shillings they had been offered. After wandering many days and running short of food, the brothers at last came to the place they were looking for. They built a log cabin and sent for their family and friends to join them. The log cabin had to serve as a home for the family, the first Post Office, the Court House and the Community Centre.

James T. Gifford was a man of great vision. He used his skill as a surveyor to plan the post road between Chicago and Galena to pass through Elgin. He laid plans for his town and used his skill as a born leader to carry these through. In an address given by Mr. Gifford in January 1850, he explained why he named his town Elgin.

"To the name Elgin, Ladies and Gentlemen, I had selected before leaving New York, for whatever point I might pitch upon, provided it had no name. I can hardly account to you for the partiality I had for the name, except it be from admiration of the tune bearing it, a tune which a celebrated critic pronounces "one of the sweetest of Scotia's Holy Lays". I had been a great admirer of that tune from boyhood and the name Elgin had ever fallen upon my ear with musical effect. This name I had selected for a Post Office and village in New York, but finding a Post Office was established in that state of that name, I had substituted Dundee and kept Elgin in reserve for this".

The softer American accent changed the hard 'g' in Elgin to a softer 'j' and that is how the name was pronounced 'Eljin' when Mr. Gifford named his town.

James T. Gifford

James T. Gifford died on August 10th 1850, a victim of Asiatic Cholera, but he left behind him the foundation of a vibrant, growing city which is Elgin today.

The base of Elgin's industrial growth was the mill race and dam which was built in 1837. Sawmills and a mill were soon to follow and with the establishment of the Elgin Watch Company in 1867, the seal was set for the town's industrial development. The Watch Company closed in 1966, but the Company's influence on the city is still evident.

From 1860–1910 Elgin was the centre of the dairy produce industry. The Elgin Board of Trade set the price of butter for the whole nation. Gail Borden set up a condensed milk factory which at its peak was using 40,000 quarts of milk daily. The Gail Borden family left a great legacy to their city. They set up the Gail Borden Library, which is thought to be one of the oldest and finest in the state.

Good planning has helped give Elgin a middle-class look unusual in an industrial city. 75% of all housing is owner occupied and one thousand acres of prime land is turned over to parks and playgrounds. The Fountain Square Plaza with its brick paved pedestrian walkway attracts many shoppers from a wide area. Over the past decade, Elgin's retail sales have exceeded 400 million dollars.

Fountain Square Plaza *Courtesy of the Daily Courier News, Elgin Illinois*

Aerial view of downtown area 1984 — *The Daily Courier News, Illinois*

The spiritual needs of the people are well catered for by 74 churches of all creeds.

Recreation covers a wide spectrum of sports. An annual event held each Memorial Day is the ten-mile Valley Fox Trot, which attracts nearly 1,000 athletes. Golf is also a very popular sport with six courses located within a few miles of the city. The Y.W.C.A. and the Y.M.C.A. provide excellent facilities for all the family to enjoy sport at a reasonable cost in beautiful surroundings.

Music and the performing arts are well supported and the Hemmens Memorial Building houses a first-class Auditorium. The city has its own 75-piece Symphony Orchestra, an active Choral Union and also theatre groups and the ballet. The Elgin area Arts Council sponsors art for young people and an art week and also publishes a calendar listing the area's cultural events.

Young people are given the advantage of a good education in the city's 33 elementary, 8 Junior High and 2 Senior High schools and nearly 90% of all students go on to some form of Higher Education. The Elgin Community College has a varied curriculum and attracts many students from the surrounding area.

Today the city is considered to be the service centre for the surrounding communities, supplying sanitation, water and transportation services along with hospital, professional offices and sheltered care home facilities.

Elgin residents are from a variety of ethnic, religious and socio-economic backgrounds and the population has reached 65,000.

In the words of Mike Alft, a former Elgin Mayor:

"Elgin is still growing, expanding as an industrial and service centre, providing opportunities for all kinds of people, some of them disadvantaged, to share the American dream".

ELGIN, MANITOBA, CANADA
1982
Margaret Robbins

The village of Elgin is located in the south-west corner of the Province of Manitoba, 35 miles north of the International Peace Garden and 50 miles from the Saskatchewan border.

This area is the beginning of the Great Western Plains, endless miles of flat land dotted here and there with groves of trees and cut by ravines. These are "the prairies", with their far horizons, excellent soil and rugged climate. Much of it is semi-arid and only the fortunate timing of rainfall prevents it from being a barren, wind-swept desert. The soil is rich and black, the best for wheat growing, hence the Elgin area is certainly part of the "bread basket of the world".

The climate of the plains is capricious and cruel. Winters are long and very cold; summers are short and unbearably hot. Temperatures range from an extreme − 35F in the winter to + 105F in the summer with frequent strong winds in both seasons, causing howling blizzards in the winter and dust storms during the dry seasons. The annual precipitation in this region averages 12″. There are fluctuations in the rainfall from year to year, causing near-drought conditions.

Several factors led to the development of Elgin, with the railways playing an extremely important role in the opening of the prairies for agriculture, and are still vital to the life of the small towns situated along their lines. We in Elgin are very fortunate that our track was not one to be abandoned in the last few years. The hard bargaining of many farmers and the grain companies played an important part in retaining this line. The railway reached Brandon in 1882 and the surrounding areas experienced a period of very rapid growth. When the first settlers arrived at this time, most of them walking the 50 miles from Brandon, they found miles and miles of grass, no roads, bridges, towns or other signs of civilization. They built sod shanties, broke the land with oxen, planted wheat and dreamed of the day when there would be schools and churches nearby. The grain grown was hauled to Brandon by oxen or horses and supplies brought back. This was a two-day trip, with stops at farms along the way for rest, refreshment and more important, the news of other settlers. Most of the settlers arriving at this time were from the British Isles.

The railway came through the present site of Elgin in 1898 and in 1899 the village of Elgin was incorporated. The name "Elgin" was given to the town by the railway company and was named after James Bruce, 8th Earl of Elgin, 1811–1863. By 1900 the population was approximately 300, with 34 places of business.

In 1903 the first school was built. As the rural population decreased, the school district was enlarged and Souris Valley School Division was formed in 1967.

As the years went by the decreasing population and higher costs of education have forced the schools in the division to combine. This has meant that Elgin High School pupils have to be bussed to Hartney Collegiate, a distance of 14 miles. Now we have grades 1-6, with two teachers for 33 pupils.

Religion is an important facet of every community's development and Elgin was no exception. Church services were held in the early years in settlers' homes and country schools until 1900, when Knox Presbyterian was built and served until union with the Methodist church in 1925. In 1904, St. John's Anglican church was opened and the same church is worshipped in today. In 1906, Grace Methodist church was built and, following union, became Elgin United Church. In 1910 the Baptist church opened its doors, and both these congregations remain active in their faith.

Recreation in the district has changed very little over the years. In the early years, cricket and lacrosse were popular with competition between neighbouring towns being quite keen. Curling has always been one of the most popular sports. The annual bonspiels have been and continue to be the highlight of the winter. The entire community takes part, either on the ice or in the kitchen. Walking into the rink and smelling the home-cooked meals and hearing the chatter and laughter coming from the kitchen portrays the spirit that has kept this community growing together.

Elgin has the same problems as most prairie towns — dwindling population as farms become larger and there are many empty farm buildings. At one time each half section supported a family; now, each farmer works two or three sections, with some of the larger farmers managing seven sections. The area around the town has changed from mixed farming to solely grain farming. In early years not a farm was without livestock; now only two large cattle farms remain. These cattlemen specialize in purebred stock, Hereford and Simmental. The main crops grown here now are wheat, barley, rapeseed, flax and sunflowers with experimental fields of corn, lentils and other special crops.

The next few years will see several farms honoured as Centennial farms as descendants of the families that originally homesteaded the land still own it. In that 100 years the changes which have taken place would be impossible for the first settlers to imagine: from oxen to horses, to steam engines, to gas-powered tractors, to diesel tractors, to the 300 horse power 4-wheel drive monsters that are common now.

At the present time there are twelve businesses in Elgin. The population is now 157 in town and 245 in the district. Many new homes have been built in the last five years, and within the last 20 years a new skating rink, curling rink

Elgin, Manitoba

and beautiful community hall have been erected entirely by volunteer labour. Elgin is serviced by sewer and an excellent water supply piped from a well outside town. Although we no longer have a resident doctor, hospital facilities are only 15 minutes away on paved and well-maintained highways. These highways also provide access to larger shopping centres.

A new grain elevator is presently being constructed, with a capacity of 110,000 bushels. It has a 70-foot scale and two legs so that grain can be taken in at the same time as railway cars are being loaded. The volume of grain handled by the two grain companies in Elgin exceeds one million bushels.

The future of Elgin is limited only by man. Her greatest asset is her people. They are the ones who tamed the West; they have known many hardships and their strength of character shows. They have a spiritual strength, a loyalty to their country and a deep sense of pride and honour. With all these resources, both human and material, the future of Elgin, Manitoba, Canada, is very promising.

ELGIN IN SOUTH AFRICA
Douglas H. D. Moodie

Elgin is situated within 50 miles of Cape Town in the South Western Cape, at latitude 34,08 South and longitude 19,02 East and lies in a basin at approximately 1,000 feet above sea level. It is almost completely surrounded by mountains, the highest of which is about 5,300 feet above sea level. The average rainfall is 39 inches (1,000mm) of which only about 10 inches fall during the summer months from November to the end of March. During the winter months the mountains are often covered in snow which, however, never lasts more than a few days.

According to records found in the Deeds Office in Cape Town, a certain Robert James Riches bought a farm in this district on 14 August 1888 and gave it the name of "Glen Elgin".

Fourteen years later, on 2 August 1902, a railway was constructed from Cape Town and where it crossed a portion of this farm a station and post office were built and given the name Elgin.

Elgin, South Africa

Elgin is the most important apple growing area in South Africa, accounting for almost half the total apples exported to the United Kingdom, Europe and North America. The high quality of the fruit is ascribed to the very suitable climatic conditions that prevail and to the highly scientific methods that are used on most farms.

The low summer rainfall has to be augmented by artificial rain in the form of under-tree sprinkler irrigation. Water is stored during the winter months in many privately owned dams which, together hold about 7,000 million gallons of water. In 1976 another very large scheme was constructed by all the farmers of this district, called the Eikenhof dam. This has a capacity of about 5,000 million gallons and feeds over 100 farms. There are over 60km of pipelines leading water to these farms. This new scheme has cost in the region of two million pounds and can irrigate an additional 7,000 acres of fruit trees. The sizes of the farms vary from 15 acres to 1,500 acres. The soil is on average only about three feet deep, consisting of a gravelly loam. In most orchards the trees are planted fairly close to each other in order to obtain the highest production possible.

It was only after the 1914/1918 World War that fruit growing in Elgin really got going. Men with good business experience came from Cape Town and elsewhere in South Africa and started growing fruit, chiefly apples. These pioneers were followed by immigrants in the form of ex-army and ex-navy Britishers in 1920 who settled in Elgin. Within a few years others followed them and Elgin rapidly became an area which took on a very English countryside atmosphere. It was largely due to these early pioneers with their expertise, foresight and determination that gradually a very important fruit exporting industry was established.

In addition to the main crop of apples, other deciduous fruit like pears, peaches, plums and nectarines are also grown. There are a few farms that practice mixed farming which includes sheep, pigs and dairying in addition to producing fruit. More recently, Oak Valley Farm has, in addition to fruit growing, also established the biggest chrysanthemum production under glass in South Africa and on another farm in Elgin, Duncan Henderson has made a name for himself in establishing one of the best rose nurseries in the country.

Less than a hundred years ago this area was considered worthless from an agricultural point of view and as a result only a handful of people lived here trying to make a living by raising cattle and sheep, but without success.

At the outbreak of the Second World War, export activities came to a halt, while along with thousands of other volunteers from all over South Africa all eligible young men left Elgin to join the struggle, some in the Air Force, others in the Navy and many in the Army. Some did not return. Many of those in Elgin who were not eligible to join Britain in her struggle nevertheless were able to play their part in another way. They threw open their Elgin homes to members of the British armed forces who passed through Cape

Town on the way to or back from the war zones in the Middle East or Far East. The many letters received from grateful members of the forces who were lucky enough to get away for a few days leave to be spent in the countryside in the orchards in Elgin, bear testimony to the kindness shown by the locals to their kith and kin who found themselves six thousand miles from their homes in Britain. It is interesting to note that Princess Alice was a regular visitor to Elgin. She used to spend a few days each year with her great friend, Miss Kathleen Murray, who was one of the earliest pioneers in this district.

There are many different religious denominations in the area, but the four main ones are Anglican, Dutch Reformed, Moravian and Roman Catholic, all of which have fine churches with resident priests. Without exception, the attendances at these and other churches are quite phenomenal and the number of worshippers is growing at a fast rate.

The total population of the area is about 15,000, made up of Whites, Coloureds and Africans. There is no doubt that this area was put on the map by the highly successful production of apples. Were it not for this fact, the area could not possibly support anything like the present population as the climate and soil is not really suitable for any other form of agriculture.

African type huts in Elgin, South Africa

NOTE: Douglas H. D. Moodie has been an apple farmer for more than fifty years in Elgin, South Africa. His great-grandfather, Capt. Benjamin Moodie, emigrated to South Africa from Melsetter, Orkney Isles, in 1817, bringing with him 200 Scottish families in three chartered ships, viz. "Brilliant", "Clyde" and "Garland". Some of these families settled in towns and on farms not far from this Elgin.

19

ELGIN, TEXAS, U.S.A.

Elgin, Texas is the only Elgin in the United States to pronounce its name the proper way, with a hard 'G'. The town was named for Robert Morris Elgin, Land Commissioner for the Houston and Texas Central Railroad and his nephew John E. Elgin stressed the pronounciation of the name saying, "There is one thing in which I desire to solicit your co-operation, that is, to give the name its proper pronounciation. There are many people who will pronounce the last syllable "gin" as liquor gin, while the proper pronounciation is as you would pronounce the word "begin". We would like in Texas to keep the correct Scotch pronounciation as the family used it."

Robert Elgin was born in Smith County, Tennessee on the 24th September, 1825 and at the age of sixteen travelled to Texas and settled in Washington County near Brenham, where he served as deputy town clerk. Following the Mexican War in which he served under General Zachary Taylor, he took up a new post as chief clerk in the General Land Office in Austin. In 1865 he became the land commissioner of the Houston and Texas Central Railroad and in 1891 retired from the railroad to enter private business. Mr. Elgin was a faithful member of the Episcopal Church and before his death on the 9th July, 1913 served as Grand Master of the Grand Lodge of Texas and Grand Commander of Knights Templars. He is buried in Glenwood Cemetery, Houston.

Robert Morris Elgin

The Deed of Dedication from the Rail Directory naming the town site Elgin is dated 18th August 1872 and the incorporation of the town of Elgin was approved by the State Legislature on the last day of May, 1873.

Small businesses were soon to flourish all over town. Wagon yards were built at the back of some stores in the early days, and families who lived several miles out of town, would camp overnight giving them a chance to meet friends and turn the collecting of stores into a social occasion.

By 1900 the population of the town had risen to 1258 and it was decided that Elgin should become a city. An election was held and a Mayor, five Aldermen and a Marshall were elected. Prior to this election law enforcement had been carried out by officers from Bastrop County.

An infestation of boll weevil in the cotton crop in the early 1900's led to a slowing down of growth but by 1910 the city was again prospering and people from the surrounding area were settling in the city, building houses and establishing new businesses.

One rather unusual business which was to prove profitable for a young man named Roy (Dutch) Frazier in 1915, was snake farming. This enterprizing young man kept his snakes in pens, feeding them meat, and when they were big enough he sold them for 25 cents the pound. The snakes were processed into snake oil for medicinal purposes.

A rich supply of red clay was considered to be a great natural resource, and from as far back as 1882, when Thomas O'Connor first sold his own hand pressed bricks, brick making has been an important industry in the city. One hundred years on in 1972 the brick plants were employing 500 men with a daily output of 770,000 brick equivalent. Elgin bricks have been exported to many countries worldwide. The National Airport and the Governor's Palace in Mexico City are but two famous places to be built with Elgin bricks.

Through the years the everyday history of the city has been faithfully recorded in the Courior. J. O. Smith and his father Dr. W. C. Smith bought the Courior in 1901 and until he retired in 1948 and moved to Bastrop, J. O. Smith was a leading citizen of Elgin. He was the first man to be named Most Worthy Citizen and he was also the first president of the Chamber of Commerce. As a city councilman he helped to bring water to Elgin and encouraged the organizing of a fire brigade. He also used his influence in securing a car park, High School, Post Office, Hospital and Elgin's Memorial Park.

During the Second World War the town bulged with servicemen and their families from the nearby Camp Swift. Rationing came into effect and everyday items such as sugar, coffee, canned and processed foods, meats, edible fats and oils, cheese and canned fish were rationed, also gasoline, tyres and shoes. Many young people joined the war effort, some were never to return to their native land.

Following the war growth was steady and by 1980 the population figures increased to 4535.

The Christian Church has always been important to the people and today there are nineteen churches in Elgin, which for many years has been known as the "Community of Churches."

The city's greatest natural resource is its people who are made up of six ethnic groups, Anglo-American, Negro, German, Mexican, Swedish and Czech and they have lived and worked together to make their city a place they are proud to bring their children up in. High on their list of priorities is education which in the early days was carried out by private schools and the church. By 1917 the school system was catering for the needs of 444 White, 222 Negro and 35 Mexican students in three separate schools but by 1965 the school system became integrated, bringing to a close the long history of separate but equal education. All children are catered for in the city education plan, which includes specialist teachers for the special child. The community plan for their childrens' future and stand proudly with their children when they sing their school song;

"Firm together stand
Comrades true and faithful
Stand a league—we'll face the world so fearlessly
And true, the days that follow.
We'll pledge our loyalty.

ELGIN, TENNESSEE, U.S.A.

Elgin is located in Scott County, Tennessee. According to the 1979 Rand McNally Commercial Atlas it has a population of 200 and its elevation is 1414 feet above sea level.

ELGIN, ALABAMA, U.S.A.

Located in Lauderdale County, Elgin has a population of 300. The place is called Elgin Cross Roads or sometimes just Cross Roads.

ELGIN, PENNSYLVANIA, U.S.A.

The village of Elgin is situated thirty miles from Lake Erie and around three hundred and fifty miles from the Atlantic ocean. The weather in summer is very hot and the winters very cold with heavy falls of snow.

The first name of the village was Hall Town, after a man named Hall who built a sawmill on the creek. With the coming of the railroad the name was changed to Concord Station but in 1876 the place was made into a borough and named Elgin. Some old people remember hearing from their fathers, that a man named Elgin lived in the village and think the village may have been named after him.

The area surrounding Elgin was settled by the McCray family and there are still many McCrays in the district. The family are of Scottish/Irish descent and the early settlers were Jesse, Jacob and James McCray.

The village has its own council and Mayor and the population is around 275.

Town Hall, Elgin, Penn. Years ago the jail was located in the basement; only two people were ever known to be lodged there

ELGIN, NEBRASKA, U.S.A.
Madonna L. Gregor

In 1883 among the earlier settlers of West Cedar Valley was Mr Wm. Eggleston of Elgin, Illinois. He located on a farm two miles north of the present site of Elgin. Eggleston soon circulated a petition for the establishment of a country Post Office, at his residence. The petition was granted by the Postal authorities and the Post Office was named Elgin after Elgin, Illinois, the place from where Mr Eggleston and family had immigrated.

In 1886, three years later, the Fremont Elkhorn and Missouri R.R. extended their Scribner line from Albion to Oakdale. They located the townsite where Elgin now stands and it was named after the Elgin Post Office. Mr. Eggleston immediately moved his family and his residence and the Post Office to the R.R. site.

It was on the 4th July, 1887 that the village of Elgin is said to have been born. Since then many businesses have come and gone and yet Elgin continued to grow and hold its own. Elgin has three churches and three schools, a nice business district, an active Chamber of Commerce, a Fire Department and Rescue Squad who are known for many miles for their quickness and ability, Legion, V.F.W., K. of C., Lodge and many more organisations too numerous to mention. Elgin's schools have had winning teams in all sports and speech and music.

Each year in June the Chamber of Commerce sponsors "Vetch Days" with a barbecue that feeds 2000 or more people. Elgin is known as the Vetch Capital of the nation. Vetch is a small black seed about the size of a b-b and is sown with rye to build up the soil. At one time Elgin shipped out more vetch from its three elevators than any other town in the nation and so became known as the Vetch Capital of the Nation. Vetch was shipped to all parts of the world.

ELGIN, CLARENDON, JAMAICA
Delseta Fearon

Elgin is located in the Parish of Clarendon, which is in the county of Middlesex and is situated towards the southern section of the island. Elgin is situated in the north central section of Clarendon, the neighbouring districts delimiting the area are Blackwoods, Thompson Town, Windsor and Main Ridge. The main town to Elgin is Chapelton, which is twelve miles away.

Elgin is a very large property which was owned by a good man named Father John Elgin. It was originally a sugar plantation in the days of slavery, when adults and children were compelled to work on the land, these were African slaves who were the only people to settle in the area. Later when Father Elgin started to advance in age, he sold off his property in small holdings to peasants of the area. Most of the properties were bought by a man named Mr. Peck. By this time the slave trade had almost ended and the new owners used their land for cultivation. They still cultivated sugar cane and set up their own horse-drawn boiling house as in the days of slavery. Father Elgin did not live very long after he sold his property and as a mark of respect the people who bought his land named the area Elgin. For a time after the death of Father Elgin, the area was inhabited by poor people, only a few could afford to buy land but those that bought allowed those that could not buy to work part of their land.

Later on the area became more popular, several houses were built and more people came to settle in the district. Today farming is carried out on a larger scale, the soil is mostly loam, a mixture of sand, clay and humus. The main crops to be found are sugar cane, bananas, cocoa, yams and citrus fruits. The people also rear animals such as pigs, cows, goats and chickens to help make a living. There are donkeys and mules to help take the crops from inaccessible areas to market and horses only used for the drawing of sugar cane mills.

Over the years Elgin prospered, a primary school was built and also a church. The villagers saw the need of a driving road and asked permission to build same, permission was granted and the road was built with local manpower. People came from the more remote districts and settled near to the road. Vehicles were now able to go in and out of the community and the villagers found it much easier to get their products to market. Elgin now has a Postal Agency which is situated in the village square.

There are eight hundred people living in Elgin, with children outnumbering adults, the population consists mainly of grand-parents and their grand-children, this is so because many of the young people have gone out to seek employment in other parishes. The residents of Elgin are mostly skilled workers, masons, carpenters, tailors and dressmakers etc. There are a

25

few teachers in the area and the children are taught to medium level. The community have no local law enforcement, so protection is provided by a district constable, whose job is made easy by law abiding people.

When someone dies in the community, the people set aside their work and get together at the house of the deceased, where they stay awake all night, singing, praying and reading scripture lessons, some dig the grave whilst others make the coffin, the women provide the tea, coffee and bread.

There is a beautiful waterfall in the community of Elgin, it is on the Thomas River, the only river that runs through the area. The river is the centre of many activities; the people in the community use it to wash clothes, bathe and get water to drink and water their animals. People from the neighbouring districts also use it to wash clothes and bathe. On holidays and weekends young men especially spend hours at the waterfall swimming. One section of the waterfall is a large circle of water which is used for baptisms.

Although Elgin is in a remote area of Jamaica it is always being recognised by visitors.

Life can be hard at times, but regardless of this the people of Elgin are happy and trust in God to see them through.

The Elgin Primary School, Jamaica with the Baptist Church in top background

ELGIN, MINNESOTA, U.S.A.

Elgin Township is well situated in the part of southeastern Minnesota known as Greenwood Prairie. It is one of the two most southern townships in Wabasha County, Plainview being the other.

The first settlers in this immediate vicinity were George Bryant, Henry Atherton, Curtis Bryant and George Farrar, who landed from a steamboat at Winona, came across that county to St. Charles and then found their way onto the borders of the rich Greenwood Prairie arriving about April 8, 1855.

The early settlers with the exception of George Farrar, came directly from Vermont. On April 21, 1855 three of the original settlers staked the claim for their future farms. Immediately after securing his claim George Bryant returned to Vermont for his family, returning in May accompanied by Leonard Laird and his family. Mrs. Bryant and Mrs. Laird were the first women in the community.

The year 1856 did much to justify the high hopes entertained by these good people. The rich soil gave promise of abundant crops and a fair acreage of land was broken up and planted. More cabins were erected, also shacks for the cattle and even a few fences constructed. The cabins were for the most part over-crowded, one small single room cabin sometimes accommodating several good-sized families of parents and growing children plus lodging for a few visiting friends. It seemed imperative that there should be a special place for the lodging of travellers and land seekers. To supply this need George and Waldo Farrar erected on the northwest quarter of section 28, the first frame house in the township. This house opened as a tavern and continued to entertain travellers till 1860. Waldo Farrar was later to be killed at the Battle of Gettysburg.

On May 11, 1858, a meeting was held for the purpose of town organization and the election of town officers. At this meeting the town was named. The whole number of votes cast was fifty-four, fifty being in favour of Elgin. Who suggested the name or why is in doubt.

The first settlers came from the eastern states where fruits were plentiful and preserves were considered as a necessary part of the daily diet. It was natural therefore that they should consider with interest the possibility of growing their own fruit.

A pioneer in fruit growing was I. W. Rollins of Elgin. Before leaving Vermont he arranged to have some apple seeds sent to him at Wabasha. These seeds were planted in the town of Elgin on April 11, 1856. The trees wintered well the first winters and in 1858 he top grafted some of them with shoots with scions from Vermont. In 1859 he and his brother planted another orchard. Some of the trees were grafted but a portion of the grafted tops were winter killed. In seven years a few trees bore fruit and in 1871 no less than 200

27

bushels were harvested. In the meantime others had become interested. There were naturally many discouragements, some of the varieties were unsuited to the climate but the pioneers did not give up and were duly rewarded. There was a great demand for their apples in Elgin and some of the bigger orchards were able to sell to outside markets.

The town grew and prospered and by 1980 the population of Elgin was 667 and growing.

ELGIN, and PORT ELGIN, NEW BRUNSWICK, CANADA

Elgin in Albert County was once a very prosperous and quite large community, but today the village is very small and relies on outside employment for its inhabitants. The village has no local offices such as Mayor or Town Clerk but there is a Justice of the Peace and a Post Office. The village has been in existence since the late 1700's.

The other Elgin in New Brunswick is Port Elgin, which is located in Westmorland County, on the banks of the River Gaspereaux. On the 22nd January, 1922 the village achieved the status of an incorporated village.

The roots of the village go back to 1836 when the village was known as Gaspereaux, the name was later changed to honour Lord Elgin.

In the beginning, the fishing industry was very important; there were so many fish in the river that when the large shoals passed down river, the river would rise several inches. Pollution of the river by the sawmills put an end to the fishing and the river became clogged with sawdust. The chief industry of Port Elgin at this time was ship building, which was carried out successfully for many years.

In 1920 the population of the village reached 1100 and the village experienced full employment, however with the coming of the depression of the 1930's businesses began to close and with no new businesses starting up the village went into a decline.

1972 found the village celebrating the 50th anniversary of the village's incorporation and under the energetic leadership of David Jones, New Brunswick's youngest Mayor, the villagers seemed determined that things could only get better, and they would no longer look back at their prosperous past but forward to a revitalized future.

28

ELGIN, IOWA, U.S.A.
Hulda Smith

A creek empties into the Turkey River in Pleasant Valley Township, Fayette County of Northeast Iowa, U.S.A. A valley of rich land is cradled between these streams, which are bordered by beautiful tree-covered hills.

Centuries ago this was a favourite burial site for many Indian tribes. As the white man planted and cultivated this area, human bones were ploughed up for many years. Thus it became known as Shin Bone Valley.

Early names of men to gain government titles to land here were Conner, Diamond, Forbes and Burdick, the surveyor. In 1848, Burdick surveyed the area and named it Elgin, after his home town, Elgin, Illinois.

The railroad built in 1874, chose not to dip into the fork of the valley to Elgin, but laid the rail line one mile west. Here another cluster of business places sprung up around the railroad depot. They named this Lutra.

Later a half-way mark was chosen for the valley school-house. An impressive large brick building was put here for all grades, from one through to high school. It was built in 1875. New homes built by retired farmers soon closed the gaps. Today, 1982, the depot is gone and Lutra is called West Elgin.

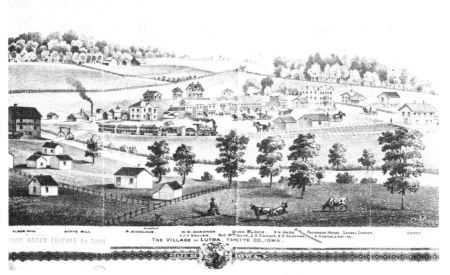

West Elgin (Lutra) in 1874

29

Road side signs along the highways leading to Elgin read thus:

"Elgin, Capitol of the Switzerland of Iowa", so chosen for the scenic views of the area and that many of the population of 702 are of Swiss and German descent. These early Swiss immigrants chose to settle south of the river among German-speaking neighbours. At the same time Scandinavians chose to cluster north of the river. Thus the first house of worship north of the river was the Norwegian Lutheran Church in the village of Gunder. South of the river the Apostolic Christians built their house for worship. Here all Sunday School classes and worship services were conducted in German. Many could speak no other language. World War 1 brought drastic changes to this community. It was considered Anti-American to speak German. Your author remembers when the government forbade sermons delivered in German. This was a sad decree for the elderly. They felt sure God would not fully understand their prayers uttered in broken English. Today, seventy-some years later, only a few senior citizens speak Swiss, German or Norwegian.

Hulda Smith, former Mayor and one of the few senior citizens who speak Swiss

30

A major industry which flourished in Elgin for some one hundred past years was the canning of locally grown sweet corn. This company is presently studying ways and means of converting corn to fuel alcohol. Improved highways forced the local railroad line out of business. Much of the surplus corn grown in Iowa today is shelled and trucked to the Mississippi River, where it is loaded on barges at the mouth of that mighty river for export to foreign lands.

Another recently terminated plant in Elgin is the Farmer's Creamery. The era 1860 to 1970, every farmer kept a small herd of cows. The milk was run through a mechanical separator as it came from the cows. Skim milk was fed to the pigs. The cream was cooled. The Creamery Company provided hauliers who picked up the cream; at the creamery it was churned into a superior quality butter.

Pure food laws affected this industry. Today the trend is to large dairy herds. Specialized operations must pass government inspection. Whole milk is picked up daily in stainless steel tankers and hauled to processing plants.

All phases of farming are becoming specialized. One operator may specialize in pork, beef, wool, a type of poultry, or a kind of grain to name a few.

These changes promote larger farming units. In some communities it lessens the close relationship between the farmer and the merchant.

The Elgin Community enjoys many events which keep the producer and the merchant working together. All club and church memberships still come from all walks of life.

A three-day Home Coming celebration held every five years involves every man, woman and child covering the school district and far beyond.

Sweet Corn Day is an annual event. The Elgin Community Club sponsors a free evening feast to the public, "All the corn-on-the-cob you can eat". As it comes from the cookers it is dipped in hot creamery butter. Long tables supplied with salt and pepper shakers provide seating.

A local church has a fund raising concession. They serve meat sandwiches, pie, cake, ice cream and coffee or soft drinks as a supplement to the free corn feast.

A program of home talent music in the bank shell adds to the fun. This all takes place in Elgin's business district city park.

A school consolidation programme swept Iowa in 1948. Rural one-room schools were closed. Highways being improved, all children were bussed to area towns. Elementary grades now occupy the Elgin school building. New buildings, centrally located in a rural setting serve high school, grades 9 to 12 for the towns of Elgin, Wadena and Clermont. The high school is accredited, which means all graduates are eligible to enter any college of their choice.

The high school offers these extra-curricular activities: band, vocal music, drama, baseball, football, basketball, track and wrestling.

Mayor Wm. Pfister, Elgin, Iowa at time
of writing

Elgin's governing body consists of one Mayor and five Councilmen. They meet twice a month with an occasional special session. Appointed officials include: City Clerk, Fire Chief, Library Board, Marshall, Cemetery Board and City Treasurer.

The town supports four churches: Baptist, Methodist, Lutheran and Apostolic. Elgin Catholics drive three miles to their church in Clermont.

Many people visit Elgin, Iowa in the fall to view the beautiful maple trees. These colourful trees lend a warmth to the landscape which is equally matched by the warm welcome the people extend to all visitors.

ELGIN, OHIO, U.S.A.

This village is one of the smaller Elgins, according to the 1970 census the population of the village was 89.

The history of Elgin starts around 1835 when Jonathan Van Eman bought land in the area which was to become Elgin, a part of York Township in the county of Van Wert. At this time the place was named Yorktown but the railroad people objected to this name as there was another Yorktown further down the line. The name was therefore changed to Elgin and incorporation was recorded on April 14, 1897.

For a short time at the end of the 19th century and the beginning of the 20th the population swelled to 300, this was due to a short oil boom. During this time the town had quite a reputation as a wide open town, it boasted three hotels, three saloons and a dance hall.

The first two-room school was established in 1897 and when the oil boom was over in 1905 the village joined the York Township school system.

In 1883 the Chicago and Atlantic Railroad ran a passenger service through the village, four passenger trains a day plus freight trains. Today the line is owned by the Erie-Lackawanna who run only freight trains.

At one time there were three churches in the village but at present only the United Brethren hold services.

There are a few flourishing family businesses in trucking and storage bin services in the village also a store and Post Office.

Village business is conducted by the Mayor, Council Clerk, treasurer and six council members. Elgin may be small but to the people of Elgin, Ohio small is beautiful.

ELGIN, NORTH DAKOTA, U.S.A.

The first name of the village was Shanley but when the Milwaukee Railroad came through in 1910 the villagers were asked to change the name as it sounded too much like Stanley which was another village down the line. A meeting of the villagers was called but they could not agree to a name, then one man looked at his Elgin watch and proposed the name Elgin. In 1978 a tornado severely damaged the village and killed five people. The population in 1980 was 930.

ELGIN, GISBORNE, NEW ZEALAND
Iris Thomas

When Elgin School celebrated its 25th Jubilee it brought into prominence the man who played a leading hand in the development of the area and established a link with a town of the same name in Scotland.

He is Robert Charles MacDuff Birrell, a Scottish immigrant who was born in Glasgow and who at the age of 36 years left his job as a railway clerk and came to New Zealand in 1891 with his wife and his family of six daughters one of whom, Jessie, died last year at the age of 92 years. His two sons, Victor and Oswald, were born later in Gisbourne.

Robert Charles MacDuff Birrell, resplendent in his MacDuff tartan, and his wife Jessie in a picture taken in the Millard Studio in Gisborne

On 20th September, 1893, Robert Birrell purchased the first of his land from Sir James Carroll and Wiremu Pere, an area of 66 acres, at a price of £462.2.0 and later in July, 1899 he purchased a further block of 35 acres. At one stage this property promised to become more valuable than it eventually did. The removal of the Taruhera freezing works placed that locality on a different level. Had this not happened the property would have been enhanced in value.

Since his first contact with Sir James Carroll when he made his first land purchase, Robert Birrell had remained a firm friend with him. Sir James Carroll was a Liberal Member of Parliament and Robert Birrell became a lively participant in political warfare, with his interest centering in support for Sir James Carroll's candidature for the Eastern Maori seat in the House of Representatives.

Robert Birrell became a leading figure in the Gisborne Debating Society, the Burns Society and was President of the Burns Society for some time. On one occasion while presiding at the annual Burns dinner of the society, the haggis was brought in cold due to a misadventure by the caterer, who was drunk. Mr. Birrell was most upset and announced gravely "The haggis is cauld".

He was also keenly interested in education and was a member of Matawhero School Committee. In later years he became an important figure in public life as a member of the Land Board and as a Government representative of the Harbour Board for some years.

During the First World War he was a noted figure in his efforts towards raising funds for the comforts of men in the services and from the early stages of hostilities there would have been few who devoted more time and energy in the activities of the Patriotic Association. He was later a member of the Repatriation Board for several years. Scots are jokingly noted for the tightness of their wallets but after the Great War Robert Birrell gave £10, a very large sum of money at that time, to many men who served with his sons. One son, Victor, later died at 39 as a result of having been gassed during the War.

His land was gradually sold to the Crown for development and roading and after 37 years' residence in the town and district he moved to Auckland as a result of a serious illness and the lack of medical care in Gisborne.

ELGIN, Today

Elgin School is situated in the heart of the Elgin area, a much larger area than the original land owned by Robert Birrell. It is a State Primary School with an attendance of about 270 boys and girls aged between 5 and 12 years. It is a "community" school, which means that the outside facilities, such as the baths, sports grounds and playground equipment are freely available to all in the surrounding district.

Elgin School's 25th Jubilee celebrations were opened by a march with bagpipes from the Gisborne Highland Pipe Band. Adding to the Scottish flavour, corsages were presented by a boy and girl wearing full Scottish dress, one a genuine MacDuff kilt, one of the very few within the Gisborne area. The school has also officially adopted a crest closely based on the crest of Elgin School, Scotland — our own adaption of a white dove on a background of maroon, the school colours. This crest is now being reproduced on letterhead paper, the school shield, and on most of the sports outfits.

Sports, especially team sport, plays a major and important part in any New Zealand child's life, not only to promote a child's physical development, but to encourage social awareness. Children are encouraged within the School to participate in many sports — cricket, gymnastics, swimming, netball, rugby and soccer, coached by interested parents and teachers. New Zealand is world renowned for its rugby (we think it is), through our All Blacks, but because the New Zealand soccer team succeeded in achieving a chance at the World Cup in Spain, soccer has gained a fast-growing interest, especially at Junior level amongst both boys and girls.

Two pupils of Elgin School, Gisborne on Sports Day

36

We are very proud of our weather, and it plays a major part in our tourist trade. We promote the fact that Gisborne is the "First City of the Sun", as we are the most easterly city in New Zealand, and therefore the first city in the world to see the sun.

Elgin is a suburb of Gisborne city and is served by a compact shopping centre comprising the usual amenities and also includes two Doctors and a Post Office. Recently a dental repair service was commenced. Children have free dental care up to the age of 16, but because of a fluoridated water supply and an ample supply of cheap milk (it used to be supplied free to all primary schools, but the service was discontinued due to waste and high costs) — teeth problems are diminishing rapidly.

Our own unique culture of the Maori people is being promoted, with encouragement from many sectors of Society and Government. The Maori language plays a much more important part in a child's education, especially the correct pronunciation. Unfortunately, today, many of the Maori population cannot speak their own language; because of the biased and short-sighted attitude of previous society, it was forbidden. However, many are confident they can forsee a bilingual society in the future of New Zealand.

We are often confused with Australians, possibly because of our close proximity — New Zealand being a small country and classed as insignificant on a world-wide scale.

I feel we are a unique mixture of varying characteristics and our "faults" are our advantages — our conservatism, parochialism, apathy, natural humour, friendliness, emphasis on sport, generosity are just a few to spring to mind.

ELGIN, UTAH, U.S.A.

Elgin is a small community near the town of Green River. A post office was established on 5th March 1898 but was closed down on the 19th August 1918. The population figure in 1909 reached 225 and the town boasted a post office, a bonded abstractor, a telephone system and a fruit growers association, also a modern store.

In the early days the area had some of the finest fruitland to be found anywhere and in the spring the countryside looked and smelled beautiful with the scented peach blossom. Some peaches measuring seven inches in diameter were sent back east to be exhibited. Sadly, due to late spring frosts ruining their crops, the farmers gradually left the valley and the trees were killed by extreme winter weather.

Education was carried out under the eagle eye of Miss Elberta Clark, who taught eight students in eight grades. The school was situated in a little log house in the town and the teacher rode one and a half miles on horseback to and from the school each day.

Many people from the town of Green River had never crossed the river to visit Elgin but in 1910 a bridge was built across the river and sightseers came to view the beautiful houses and orchards. People steadily moved out of the town and by 1979 there were only 50 people living in Elgin.

ELGIN, KANSAS, U.S.A.

1885 was the year of great change for Elgin, Kansas. The Cedar Vale branch of the Santa Fe Railroad was completed and the cattlemen in the Elgin area realised that their town could become the cattle centre of America.

A notice at the old stock yards reads as follows: "During a time between 1890 and 1905 this was considered the largest shipping point in the world. A government dipping vat was located in these yards, this helped to eradicate Texas fever. A turn-table to turn steam engines was located nearby. Trains backed up for miles waiting to load at the two loading chutes that operated 24 hours a day during shipping season. The yards continued in operation until 1939, when the railroad was abandoned."

The name of Elgin became established in 1890 and in 1965 the town celebrated it's diamond jubilee, with a homecoming. One of the main features of the homecoming was the opening of the Chautauqua County Historical Museum. Elginites came from all over America to celebrate their jubilee with their families and friends, dancing in the streets and enjoying a barbecue.

The people of Elgin, Kansas are proud of their past and the role they play in the growth of their country and they hope that by the year 1990 when they celebrate their centenary, they will have written yet another page in the history of the Sunflower State.

ELGIN, NEVADA, U.S.A.

In the atlas Elgin is described as rural with no population figure given and no Post Office of its own. Elgin was once an important water stop on the Salt Lake route of the Union Pacific Railroad.

ELGIN, WESTERN AUSTRALIA
James W. H. Reid

Elgin is essentially and entirely a farming district, relying on milk and beef production.

My parents, of Scottish descent, came here from Perth W. A. to farm about 1904, and I was born there in 1910. There were at the time of my parents coming, just a few scattered homes in the area. About half a mile from where we lived was the farm of the Clark family. Dorothy Clark (now Dinnie) was the daughter of the house and it was her paternal grand-father, John Clark who named the area Elgin. John Clark was born in Elgin, Scotland and came to Australia with his parents.

John Clark, born in Elgin, Scotland about 1840,
son of David Clark

At this time the few farmers living in the area, relied mainly on selling or bartering their produce in Bunbury, eighteen miles away. Bunbury was then a small town of a few thousand residents but is now a city for the area. In the early days there were very few cattle in the Elgin district. Farmers had mainly sheep, a few small orchards, and they grew potatoes and oaten crops.

The whole of the Elgin district was marked as such on an early map I have seen; but it was also known and marked "The Ronald Clark Estate". Since then this has been split up into farms of approximately 200 to 500 acres and is more intensely farmed. The land is very fertile.

In the early days of my knowledge, there were very few fences with a few roads through the bush and all transport carried out with the aid of horses which were also used for all farm work.

There has never been a shop in Elgin. The nearest shops are in Capel, five miles to the west and Boyanup six miles east. Most business is done in Bunbury which is eighteen miles away or in Perth which is 120 miles distant. The railway from Perth to Brusselton runs through Elgin.

All mail comes through post offices in Capel and Boyanup. Residents were connected by telephone about fifty years ago but electric power was only connected in the 1950's. The only public building in the district of Elgin is a small hall which is used for meetings, dances and badminton.

Everybody who has lived here has little doubt that our Elgin is one of the best farming areas in Australia.

ELGIN, LANCASTER COUNTY and ELGIN, KERSHAW COUNTY, SOUTH CAROLINA, U.S.A.

There are two Elgins in South Carolina. The elder of the two is Elgin in Lancaster County. This Elgin was formerly St. Luke, named after the St. Luke Methodist Church. When the railroad came through in 1895 the officials named the village and the Post Office, Elgin.

The younger Elgin in Kershaw County became Elgin in 1963, after bitter exchanges between the two villages. In 1962 the Elgin National Watch Company started construction of their new watch factory in the village of Blaney. The citizens of Blaney decided to change the name of their village to Elgin, to honour the watch company. A vote was taken and the villagers decided 61 votes to 16 to change the name to Elgin. The villagers of unincorporated Elgin, Lancaster were angry when they heard of Blaney's plans and registered a strong protest, but to no avail. Blaney was changed to Elgin and despite the fact that the watch company closed five years later, the village has kept the name Elgin.

ELGIN, OKLAHOMA, U.S.A.
Submitted by the History of Elgin Committee, Oklahoma

A stretch of prairie of tall blue stem, the former reservation of the Kiowa and Comanche Indians, was open to settlement in 1901. Each Indian was alloted a 160 acre tract of his or her choice, the remainder was open to others by lottery with the exception of sections 16 and 36 of every township, reserved as school land. Rolling prairie marks the site of the town, farmland intersected with creeks and small streams. Eager homesteaders poured in to buy the lots for sale and the town had an early 'boom' which has continued intermittently to the present time.

The people who rapidly moved to this area were in need of the services of a town near a shipping point. Early in 1902 the Frisco Railroad Company authorised contractors to begin work on the railroad line to extend southwest from Oklahoma City to Quannah, Texas.

One of the contractors was C. G. Jones, who was also a townsite promoter. A townsite was platted on 160 acres just north of the north east of Fort Sill Military Reservation and given the name of Cee Gee, it is said from the initials of Mr. C. G. Jones the promoter. An application for a post office made under the name of Cee Gee was rejected by the authorities because a post office of a similar sounding name had already been established in Oklahoma Territory. A citizen who had been visiting Elgin, Illinois, suggested the name Elgin for the new post office. The name was accepted by the postal department and thus post office and town received the name of Elgin. The town was incorporated in 1909. Local government is Chairman and Council and the term of office is 4 years for the Chairman and 4 Council Members.

The population of the town has risen steadily from 200 in 1902 to 1075 in 1980.

The first buildings were wooden structures, gradually replaced as the years went by and business buildings outnumbered residences. The few remaining residences have been remodelled and modernised. One old grain elevator is still in use.

In the beginning the farmers depended upon the merchants for many goods and services. Cotton was the main product of the area in the early days but today the chief products of the area are beef cattle, dairy products, hogs, poultry, fruit, potatoes and other vegetables, also mining, natural gas, petroleum, sand, gravel, and limestone.

The Wichita Mountains to the west make a picturesque setting for the homes of Elgin citizens, many of whom trace their ancestry to European heritage as well as to Indian ancestry.

41

Elgin, Oklahoma, USA

The railroad contributed greatly to the early growth of the town but the year 1984 finds very little evidence of the Frisco Railroad except for the switching tracks and the rail lines that still transport heavy freight. The energy crisis has caused attention to be focused, once again on the railroads. It remains to be seen whether the passenger train will make a comeback in Oklahoma.

ELGIN, ONTARIO, CANADA

The peaceful Rideau Lake district is the setting for the beautiful village of Elgin, Ontario.

In the year 1802 Ebenezer Halladay, a United Empire Loyalist was granted the land on which the village stands. Ebenezer was one of the many United Empire Loyalists to settle in the Rideau district after the American War of Independence.

The United Empire Loyalists were known as the King's Men and as a mark of honour they were allowed to put U.E.L. after their name. Each loyalist settler was given land according to his rank, 1000 acres to a field officer, 700 acres to every captain and to every subaltern, staff officer and warrant officer 500 acres, each non-commissioned officer received 200 acres and every private 100 acres. In addition to this a further 50 acres were granted for each member of the man's family.

Over the years the village has had three names, the first, Halladay Corners, was chosen after work on the Rideau Canal commenced in 1826 and with the upsurge of population it was decided that the village should have a name. During the 1830's many families were converted to the Mormon faith and in the year 1834 one hundred and thirty five covered wagons travelled from Halladay Corners to the Mormon settlement of Nauvoo in the United States. The village blacksmith at this time was one Harvey Mitchell; Harvey had a dream of one day joining the settlers in Nauvoo, he spoke of his dream so often that the villagers tired of hearing him and decided in jest to change the name of the village to Nauvoo. The final name of Elgin was put forward by Robert Dargavel a Scottish pioneer who wished to honour James Bruce, 8th Earl of Elgin who was the Governor-General Canada from 1847 to 1855. Since then the village has grown and prospered.

The land on which the old Methodist Church stood was gifted by Ebenezer Halladay, along with a large cash donation; this generous man also donated the land for the village cemetery, which still bears his name. Today his great-grandson Merton Campbell lives on part of the original Halladay farm land.

Farming was the main industry in the early days but in recent years the tourist industry has grown and has been a very important factor in the economic growth of the village.

Visitors are always impressed with the beautiful architecture of Elgin. Large old houses set back from the road in tree-filled gardens. The Anglican Church with its Norman tower, the stained glass of United Church and the large Roman Catholic Church are all very pleasing to the eye.

There are two schools in the village, an elementary and a secondary, and at the other end of the scale a senior citizens complex. The community have their own doctor and dentist and a thriving business section. Many of the residents commute to work in Kingston, Smith Falls and Brockville and in their spare time take part in the busy social life of the village which includes sport and an active Lions Club..

The people of Elgin, Ontario are justly proud of their village and work hard to ensure its future.

ELGIN, ARKANSAS, U.S.A.

In the early 1830's Robert T. Dunbar came to Jackson County from Mississippi to establish a plantation and on it a boarding school in Bird Township. A ferry licence was issued to him to run a ferry across the Black River at Elgin in 1836, though is is possible that the ferry was in operation for years before this date. Robert T. Dunbar was believed to be the grandson of Sir Archibald Dunbar of Duffus Castle near Elgin, Scotland. Robert died without issue in 1839 and his property was bought by Edmund James Taylor in 1873. The ferry closed in 1979 when it was replaced by a bridge.

When Jackson County Historical Society founded their museum in 1964, Miss Lucile Taylor, grandaughter of Edmund James Taylor, wrote to the Town Clerk of Elgin, Scotland, requesting some souvenir of Elgin, to place in the Jacksonport museum. Miss Taylor reported to her committee as follows: — "In response the Council had a wooden plaque carved and painted of the Coat-of-Arms of the City for exhibition in our museum. The plaque was made by the Heraldic Woodcarver to the standing council of Scottish Chiefs." Miss Taylor quoted from the accompanying letter received from Mr Harold Tait "My council agreed to present a plaque of the Coat-of-Arms of the City . . . and I have pleasure in sending it herewith. The centre-piece represents St. Giles, the Patron Saint of Elgin." The plaque is about 14″ by 18″ in size. In reply Miss Taylor sent the following letter: — "In appreciation for the interest of the Council of Elgin in its namesake here, members of the Council have been made honorary members of the Jackson County Historical Society. They will receive our quarterly publication and I have sent a box containing samples of Jackson County products to them. One product, a beautiful boll of raw cotton, has possibly never before found its way to this old friendly town in the north of Scotland, one of whose sons lies sleeping by the shore of another river, at another Elgin."

Owing to postal problems the "Stream of History" is no longer sent to Old Elgin but the Town Council of Elgin, Scotland are still honorary members of the Jackson County Historical Society.

ELGIN, ARIZONA, U.S.A.

Elgin,
October 5, 1978

"Who named Elgin, Arizona?," you ask. I'm not sure. Occasionally someone hereabouts asks the same question. It was named Elgin some time after the Benson to Nogales branch of the Southern Pacific Railroad was built. I believe that the S.P.R.R. was completed some time in the early 1880's. Elgin was one of the rare areas along the railroad right of way with ample supplies of wood and water nearby. The S.P.R.R. dug a well and erected a tank. There the trains stopped daily, taking on water and loading wood, fuel for the wood-burning locomotive. Later Elgin became a stopping point to receive and ship freight.

With no mail service nearer than Ft. Crittenden in one direction, evacuated in 1861, at the beginning of the Civil War, and Ft. Huachuca which was established in 1877, Elgin was well known as a shipping point, though no Post Office was established there until 1911.

By that time, the sparsely settled area about ten or twelve miles from Ft. Huachuca, known as Canille Canyon, established a Post Office in 1904 with a star route carrying mail daily to and from the Elgin stopping point, the Conductor receiving and delivering the mail bags.

The new land held great promise for the future. Cattle barons ran vast herds of wild cattle on open range; the miners were making millions shipping gold, silver and copper. Naturally, young men, well-educated and often men of great vision, sought their fortune in the new world.

One such young man, Colin Cameron, an unusually popular and able young official, was associated with the Greene Cattle Company. This powerful cattle company, which was interested in building a great railroad system, encouraged Colin, who chose "Elgin" as a name for the new stopping point.

In 1911, Ruben B. Collie was appointed the first Postmaster of Elgin, Arizona. By that time this mailing point had long been known as Elgin.

My tale draws to a close. The postal changes now contemplated, I understand, will close the Elgin Post Office soon.

Cora Everhart

45

I am taking the liberty of answering your recent letter to my mother, Mrs. Cora Everhart. In explanation, my mother is almost 96 years of age and although very active and capable for her age, her interest is now centred on writing up a history of the Canelo School, now defunct. Canelo had one of the earliest school districts in this part of the state. Someone that works for the Herald Dispatch newspaper at Sierra Vista, Arizona has enlisted her aid in this project.

Concerning the Elgin Post Office, the latest news is that US Postal Representatives have held a meeting with the Elgin Community citizens and informed them that the Elgin Post Office will be discontinued and the surrounding communities will then be served by rural mail routes, delivering to mail boxes. We do not know yet when this will occur.

Since your primary interest in Elgin should dominate this letter, I will try to fill in from my own recollections as my early childhood and some of my early school-years were spent in Elgin.

My first recollection of Elgin concerns the railroad, a two-storey section house for the Railroad Maintenance Foreman and his family, with a number of railroad boxcars set off their wheels as housing for the railroad section crews and their family members. Also part of the R.R. property was boxcar housing for the freight agent, and a warehouse. A well-house, pump and water tower completed the facility. All this was located east of the Elgin "creek" which was normally spring-fed pools of considerable size with water running from one to another, eventually reaching the Babacomari branch of the San Pedro River system. Beyond the railroad property was the Elgin schoolhouse. There were many large cottonwood trees in Elgin.

West of the Elgin creek was a two-storey hotel and a general store, the Post Office building (owned by my mother and father) and a large barn or stable. The building housing the Post Office was the first Post Office actually erected in the town of Elgin. The first Post Office was some two or more miles away at the home of the first post master.

The following sketch illustrates my memory of Elgin during the 1918–1924 period.

Jack Everhart

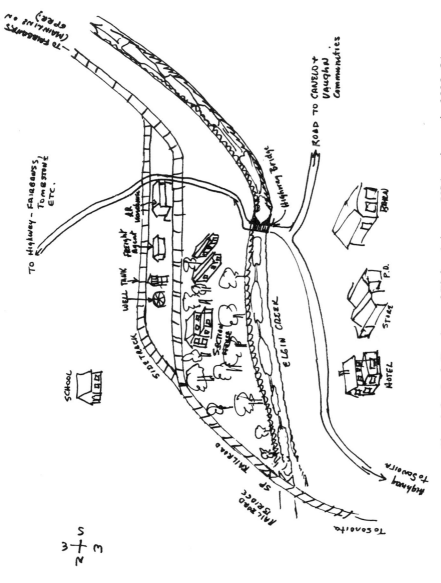

Sketch by Jack Everhart of Elgin, Arizona, USA as it was in 1918–24

The following labels appear within the sketch:

— TO FAIRBANKS (MAINLINE OR SPUR?)

ROAD TO CANELO + VAUGHN Communities

TO HIGHWAY — FAIRBANKS, TOMBSTONE ETC.

Spring Branch Bridge

Highway to Sonoita

To Sonoita

RR Agent Warehouse

Freight

WELL TANK

Section House

SIDETRACK

SCHOOL

ELGIN CREEK

SP RAILROAD

RAILROAD BRIDGE

BARN

P.O.

STORE

HOTEL

S
3 — E
N W

ELGIN, ASHBURTON, NEW ZEALAND
Violet H. Donaldson

Elgin Ashburton was named by an early settler, James Bruce.

It is described in the official county council books as a farming locality on the Wakanual Creek 6km south east of Ashburton and covers an area of approximately 6,000 acres.

My first introduction to it was in 1911 when my two brothers emigrated to New Zealand and after visiting relatives in this district wrote back to Aberdeen telling us of the wonderful crops of wheat, oats and barley and the small amount of tillage required to produce these crops. Little did I think then, that I would spend twenty five of the happiest years of my life at Elgin.

My husband bought the farm in 1946 from the late Duncan Cochrane and from him I learned something of the early days of the district. His father was one of the two boundary riders in the days when the land belonged to the Crown and both these men eventually settled in the area.

The way in which Mr. Cochrane's father chose his piece of land was to select the area which grew the biggest tussocks and the deal was concluded at the price of £2 an acre. A sod hut was built on the property and in it Duncan was born but about the turn of the century this was replaced by a four bedroomed wooden house surrounded on three sides by wide verandahs — this still stands in good order to the present day.

Elgin Farmhouse, Elgin, Ashburton, New Zealand

Mr. Cochrane was a successful sheep breeder as was evidenced by the number of prize winning tickets lining the walls of the old woolshed. He hired an experienced Scottish shepherd to help look after the flock and this man left me an unfortunate legacy which still proves a problem to the present day.

He planted ivy to provide ivy poultices for sheep foot troubles — successful it may have been, but how I cursed that ivy! It grew and spread, tenaciously clinging to the large trees lining the long drive into the property and obliterating the rhododendrons and other flowering shrubs which were planted along the side of the creek which flowed along the front and side of the house.

Mr. Cochrane and his sister were also responsible for planting the blue gum trees on the farm. They carried water from the Ashburton river almost a mile away to nurture these trees in their early stages. Lack of water in areas of Elgin farther from the river produced an interesting experiment. The first trial irrigation in New Zealand occurred in what was known for many years as the irrigation farm. This has in recent years been replaced by an automatically activated modern system of irrigation.

In earlier years the Elgin district had a school, post office and telephone bureau but now every home can dial directly to the Ashburton telephone exchange. The children too are collected in modern buses and delivered to schools in Ashburton or Wakanui.

Because of its proximity to the Borough of Ashburton a considerable amount of subdivision has taken place. At present there are 80 separate properties in this area, with houses being built on as little as 5 acre lots. Land values have increased astronomically — present day values for farm land would be in the region of $2,000 an acre. It is still very much a farming community but a very progressive one and we are truly proud of "Our Elgin".

ELGIN, OREGON, U.S.A.
Ethel M. Smith

As late as the middle 1800's the geographic site of Elgin, Oregon, U.S.A., was Indian territory. Chief Joseph, leader of the Nez Perce Nation, has been written up in many books and stories as a leader with great dignity, honour, and truthfulness. The people of the Nez Perce migrated over a very large area in the western states of Oregon, Idaho and Washington, and into Canada. Elgin was one of their camping places before the white man settled here. They called it "Lochow Lochow" which means "lovely little forest".

And it is still lovely. A small valley, completely surrounded by protective mountains, contains the small town and its inhabitants. It is appropriately called Indian Valley. Many of the pine and fir trees that hovered over the native Americans are still growing and shading the sons and grandsons of the white men who invaded their land.

It was in 1890 that the first trains came to Elgin. They were bringing a new concept of service to the 90 families who were living here at that time. Elgin was founded in 1885. The first City Council meeting minutes on record are dated 1891.

The first freight trains were used primarily for hauling logs as this is and was a timber, logging and farming area. For years the logging camps were scattered throughout the forests for many miles around, and, because of slow transportation there was a one-room school in almost every camp. Entire families lived in the camps. Coming to town for supplies was at least a full day's journey and a real event in the lives of those early settlers.

There is a current population in Elgin of 1760. An elementary school, housing grades one to eight, and a high school for grades nine to twelve educate the local students. There is a state accredited college 20 miles away in La Grande, Oregon.

About 40 businesses compete with "big city" stores that are from 20 to 300 miles distant. Freight is now hauled by fast, efficient trucks and vans. At one time the only freight lines consisted of mule trains, 25 to 40 animals in each packer's string. They carried everything from gold dust to food to lacy lingerie for the night ladies in various mining camps and cow towns.

One innovative packer in about 1866 tried Arabian camels in this area as pack animals but they weren't satisfactory on the mountain trails, or the trail-less terrain, and they spooked the mules in another train, causing a stampede and doing great damage.

It took hardy stock to carve out a home in the Elgin area. To farm meant that tracts of land must be cleared of timber and brush. Loggers many times lived in tents and inadequate cabins and worked in below-zero weather in the winter and tinder dry heat in the other extreme.

Housewives scrubbed clothes on a washboard, carried gallons of water from the nearest stream or spring, and, like women everywhere before the turn of the century, worked extremely hard to keep their families clothed and fed, and their homes clean.

Then gradually, "Lochow Lochow" began to change its features. First, houses of planed lumber appeared in the town and on some of the more prosperous ranches. Stone was quarried on Gordon Creek, about four miles from town, and some of these stones were used in a few local structures, two of which are still in use. Also rock from that quarry was freighted to some of the eastern United States by locomotive.

Then brick buildings appeared and in 1912 and 1913 the Opera House City Hall was built. This boasted the most complete stage set and elegant interior of any theatre between Mississippi River and Portland, Oregon. The multi-purpose building is still in use, housing the city offices including the police station; and insurance office: the local theatre; and a small area utilized by the local television association. Also, the building is now listed on the National Historical Monument register in Washington, D.C.

The Elgin area is rich in history. The name itself came from the song "Lost on the Lady Elgin", a ballad which told of lives lost in a shipwreck at sea. It seems that a local father heard his two children singing the song and decided that the name 'Elgin' had a good sound to it and that it was a good name for the town. And so "Lochow Lochow" became Elgin.

There is a log barn a few miles from town on Cricket Flat that was built on July 4, 1876. The neighbours came to a barn raising that day and in one day the building was completed. Of course the ladies were there with all the fixin's for a bounteous picnic dinner and while the men worked, the women visited and the children played their many games. Everyone enjoyed the 'social gathering' and made the most of it. The barn was used as a fort during at least one Indian uprising, probably the last one in this area.

Elgin's government consists of an elected mayor and six city council members. They, like the fire department and ambulance crew, are on a voluntary basis and are not paid. There is a salaried city manager-recorder, a clerk and a police department as well as other necessary city employees.

Descendants of many of Elgin's founding fathers are still in this area. Some current names that have been around for four and five generations include Hug, Follett, Parsons, Galloway, Hindman, Rysdam and Scott, to name only a few. At least one ranch directly related to Elgin was honoured a few years ago as having been in the same family for over one hundred years.

There has been an influx in Elgin in recent years of big city people seeking a quieter, more slowly paced life. Local citizens for the most part have welcomed them and some new ideas are gradually being absorbed by the native sons and daughters. They can understand others for wanting to live here because, after all, most of them know they live in one of the most beautiful, liveable places in the world.

City Hall, Elgin, Oregon — *Courtesy, Rick Houston*

ELGIN FALLS AND ELGIN, SRI LANKA

The Elgin Falls are located in Central Province on Hatton Plateau, at altitude 6064ft. The Falls form part of the right tributary of the Mahaweli Ganda. The town of Elgin is about 3 miles away from Falls, and the most important town closest to Elgin Falls is Nuwara Eliya which is about 10 miles in distance. There are place-names such as Mornington, Glasgow, MacDuff, Edinburgh and Waverley nearby, which can be regarded as results of British administration in Sri Lanka.

On the tea estates in the main tea-growing area around Nuwara Eliya, twice as many children die before their first birthday as anywhere else in Sri Lanka.

They die from diseases which are rarely killers in Britain, such as measles, polio, diptheria, whooping cough, tetanus, tuberculosis and from diarrhoea and malnutrition.

To help this, UNICEF is promoting a vigorous programme of vaccination and encouraging estate workers to grow nutritious vegetables in home gardens.

A quarter of all children get no schooling. Even more children must earn extra money to help towards the family budget. They go to school irregularly, often dropping out altogether. Many primary schools have leaking roofs, ramshackle desks, no blackboard and few qualified teachers. Such schools are usually found in rural areas. Here again, UNICEF is helping by providing textbooks and equipment, training teachers and encouraging school gardens.

1981–1990 is the International Drinking Water Supply and Sanitation decade. With this worldwide effort to provide clean water and adequate sanitation for all by the year 1990, the hope is that a better future for the children of Sri Lanka will become a reality.

Sri Lankan children fetch water from an India Mark II handpump, designed especially for heavy use in villages.

UNICEF photo by Vivianne Holbrooke

During the Summer of 1984 the Elgin branch of UNICEF held an essay competition for school children. Part of the winners prize was to have their work printed. Jacqueline Taylor of Elgin High School and Cathryn Rees of Elgin Academy tied for first place.

SAINT GILES, PATRON SAINT of ELGIN
Jacqueline Taylor

Saint Giles was born towards the end of the 7th century and he died in the first half of the 8th century A.D. Not much is known about his early life and, in fact, most of what we are told about him is legend.

Giles was born in Athens, in Greece. According to legend he was of noble and possibly royal birth, and was 'devoted to good works from his cradle'. He left Greece and went to France, where he lived two years with Saint Caesarius at Arles. He became a hermit and spent several years living in wild desert near the mouth of the river Rhone. Then he spent some time in a forest in the diocese of Nismes.

While living in the forest, Giles is said to have lived on herbs and the milk of a hind. The hind was supposed to be sent by God to visit him daily and give him milk. The Saint's symbols, a hind and an arrow, refer to a famous legend based on a tenth century biography. Flavius, king of the Goths at that time, was hunting a hind in the forest where St Giles was living. The hind fled to Giles for safety and the King, who was giving chase, wounded Giles in the arm with an arrow. Flavius begged the saint's pardon and it was granted. Later, the King decided to build an abbey. This was done and Giles became its abbot. He later became a priest, and died in the monastery which he had ruled.

When Giles died, his body remained in Nismes till the 13th century. Then it was moved to the church of St Saturnius, in Toulouse.

Giles appears on Elgin's coat of arms, holding a book and a crozier. He is robed and mitred. This is not very accurate as Giles was never a bishop, and mitres were not even invented when he was alive. Two angels support the shield. The motto on the coat of arms is 'Sic Itur Ad Astra'. Literally translated, this means 'thus they go to the stars'. It has also been translated as 'tis thus that men to Heaven aspire' or, more commonly, as 'this is the way to immortality'. The coat of arms was registered in 1888.

SIC·ITUR·AD·ASTRA

The Saint also figures on the common seal of the Burgh of Elgin. He still carries his crozier and open book, but is dressed in a priest's robes. The seal was first mentioned in 1244.

Despite all this, no-one knows exactly why Giles was chosen to be Elgin's patron saint. Perhaps somewhere there is a legend about that, too.

MAJOR GENERAL ANDREW ANDERSON (1747-1824)
Cathryn Rees

In 1745 Marjory Gilzean married a soldier and left for India with her new husband, only to return two years later, a weak-minded, penniless widow, with a baby son in her arms. She sought shelter in Elgin Cathedral, cradling her son in the baptismal font and claiming the Chapter House as her home.

Young Andrew was well educated at the Grammar School in Elgin and was then apprenticed to his uncle, a staymaker in St. Andrews — Lhanbryde. At the age of thirteen he ran away to London to make his fortune in the tailoring trade but instead he enlisted into the Honourable East India Company as a private soldier and drummer and was consequently sent to India.

He was known to be persevering and reliable. On one occasion his division came upon a marsh. The commanding officer gave instructions to alight and lead on foot through a muddy and dirty path. The captain of the division refused. Anderson immediately sprang forward, seized the standard and led the troops forward. It is said that the £16,000 prize money which he received for his services on this occasion laid the foundation of his fortune.

It is by qualities and incidents such as this, that Anderson rose to the distinguished rank of Major-General.

After a long and distinguished career and at the age of sixty-four, General Anderson returned to Elgin where he resided for a few years, during which time he communicated with the provost and other town officials, visited old people and wandered along the banks of the River Lossie. He left for London and was not heard of again in Elgin until 1826-27 when the contents of his will were revealed.

In his will, General Anderson had bequeathed his estate of sixty to seventy thousand pounds (after certain annuities) to the Sheriff, magistrates and Clergy of the Established Church in Elgin as trustees to found, firstly a hospital for the support of elderly men and women, not under fifty-five years of age. Secondly a "School of Industry" for the support and education of male and female children of the working class and for finding apprenticeships or employment for these children and finally, a free school for the education only of male and female children whose parents can afford to feed and clothe, but not to educate them.

"The Elgin Institution for the Support of Old Age and the Education of Youth" as General Anderson specified in his will, was duly completed in 1831 at a cost of twelve thousand pounds and the initial occupants were five elderly men and a like number of women, twenty-four boys and sixteen girls, plus up to three hundred pupils attending the free school.

After their school education ceased at the age of fourteen, boys chose their desired trade or occupation and their employers were each given an annual allowance to keep the boy properly clothed and fed, girls were generally employed as domestic staff and there are many people, young and old alike, who have thanked Anderson for his posthumous gift.

Many an adolescent in the search for freedom and fortune forgets a parent; could it be that Andrew Anderson wished to ensure that at least some young people would have a better start in life than he and that a few old people would have a better end to their lives than his lonely, estranged, penniless mother? If so he has set an example that certainly we could do worse than try to follow.